I0002194

Launching things "ugly" can be a counterintuitive but effective strategy for product managers seeking rapid iteration, user feedback, and market validation.

In the fast-paced world of product development, the traditional approach of polishing a product to perfection before launch might not always be the most efficient or strategic.

This concept of launching things "ugly" involves releasing a product or feature that may not be aesthetically pleasing or fully refined but is functional enough to gather valuable insights from real users.

Embracing Imperfection

In a world obsessed with perfection and polished user interfaces, the idea of launching something "ugly" may seem risky. However, it's about shifting the focus from perfection to functionality and usability. Embracing imperfection allows product managers to overcome the fear of failure and the pressure to deliver a flawless product from the start.

Launching an imperfect product doesn't mean neglecting quality or user experience entirely. It means prioritizing the core functionalities that address users' needs and deliver value. By doing so, product managers can expedite the development process, reduce time to market, and start gathering user feedback early in the product lifecycle.

Rapid Iteration and Learning

Launching things "ugly" encourages a mindset of continuous improvement through rapid iteration. Instead of spending months or even years on perfecting a product behind closed doors, product managers can release a minimum viable product (MVP) quickly and iterate based on real user feedback.

This approach allows for a more dynamic development process, with the product evolving in response to user insights and changing market conditions. Rapid iteration enables teams to fix issues, enhance features, and adapt to user preferences swiftly, resulting in a more user-centric and market-responsive product.

User-Centric Design in Action

Launching things "ugly" aligns with the principles of user-centric design. By involving users early in the process, product managers can gain a deeper understanding of their needs, preferences, and pain points. This direct user involvement can lead to the creation of products that better meet user expectations and deliver a more satisfying user experience.

User feedback collected from the initial, imperfect launch provides valuable insights that can guide product enhancements. This iterative feedback loop ensures that the product is refined based on real-world usage, rather than theoretical assumptions or internal opinions.

Validating Ideas and Assumptions

Launching things "ugly" is a powerful tool for validating product ideas and assumptions. Instead of relying on internal brainstorming sessions or market research alone, releasing an imperfect version of the product allows product managers to test hypotheses in a real-world context.

By observing how users interact with the product and analyzing their feedback, product managers can validate or adjust their initial assumptions. This data-driven approach to product development minimizes the risk of investing significant resources in ideas that may not resonate with users or meet market demands.

Time to Market Advantage

In competitive industries, time to market can be a critical factor in a product's success. Launching things "ugly" provides a strategic advantage by allowing products to enter the market sooner, potentially capturing early adopters and gaining a foothold before competitors.

The traditional approach of refining a product to perfection before launch often results in a longer development cycle. In contrast, an "ugly" launch prioritizes speed and responsiveness, enabling product managers to capitalize on market opportunities and respond quickly to emerging trends.

Building a Culture of Innovation

Launching things "ugly" is not just a product development strategy; it's a mindset that fosters a culture of innovation within a team or organization. Embracing imperfection, encouraging risk-taking, and valuing rapid iteration contribute to a dynamic and forward-thinking work environment.

A culture of innovation is essential for staying ahead in industries where change is constant. By promoting the launch of imperfect products, product managers signal to their teams that innovation and learning from mistakes are not only accepted but encouraged.

Overcoming Perfection Paralysis

The pursuit of perfection can often lead to paralysis, where teams become stuck in an endless cycle of refinement and never reach the point of launching. Launching things "ugly" breaks this cycle by shifting the focus from achieving perfection to delivering value and learning from user interactions.

Overcoming perfection paralysis is crucial for maintaining momentum and preventing stagnation. By embracing imperfection, product managers empower their teams to take bold steps forward, learn from real-world outcomes, and continuously evolve the product.

Mitigating Resource Constraints

In many cases, product managers face resource constraints, whether it's limited time, budget, or personnel. Launching things "ugly" is a pragmatic approach to product development that acknowledges these constraints and seeks to maximize the impact of available resources.

Rather than allocating extensive resources to perfect every aspect of a product before launch, product managers can prioritize the essential features that deliver the most value. This resource-efficient approach allows for a quicker time to market and a more efficient use of available resources.

Balancing "Ugly" with User Experience

While the concept of launching things "ugly" emphasizes functionality over aesthetics, it's essential to strike a balance. User experience should not be sacrificed entirely in the pursuit of speed and efficiency. Even an "ugly" product should be intuitive, easy to use, and provide a positive user experience.

Product managers must identify the core functionalities that matter most to users and ensure that these are well-implemented. Clear communication about the product's status as an early release or MVP can also manage user expectations, fostering understanding and patience during the iterative development process.

Case Studies of Successful "Ugly" Launches

Several successful products and companies have embraced the strategy of launching things "ugly" to achieve rapid iteration, user feedback, and market validation.

One notable example is Dropbox, which started as a minimal file-sharing service with a simple interface.

The early version lacked the sophisticated features seen in later iterations but was functional and addressed a pressing user need.

Through continuous iteration based on user feedback, Dropbox evolved into a widely-used cloud storage platform.

Another example is the lean startup methodology, popularized by Eric Ries.

The lean startup approach advocates for quickly launching a minimum viable product, learning from user feedback, and iterating to improve the product.

This methodology has been embraced by numerous successful startups that prioritize speed and learning over perfection.

Conclusion

Launching things "ugly" challenges conventional product development wisdom by prioritizing functionality, rapid iteration, and user feedback over perfection.

This strategy is not about neglecting quality or user experience but about making strategic trade-offs to expedite the development process and maximize the impact of available resources.

By embracing imperfection, product managers can build a culture of innovation, overcome perfection paralysis, and gain a time-to-market advantage.

Launching things "ugly" is a mindset that aligns with user-centric design principles, enabling product managers to validate ideas and assumptions in the real world.

While the strategy may not be suitable for every product or industry, it offers a valuable alternative for those seeking agility, responsiveness, and a dynamic approach to product development.

In a world where change is constant, launching things "ugly" may be the key to staying ahead in the ever-evolving landscape of technology and innovation.

Thanks for reading. Hopefully this helps...

Here is some space for note-taking:

www.ingramcontent.com/pod-product-compliance
Lightning Source LLC
LaVergne TN
LVHW022127060326
832903LV00063B/4800